<u>The 1 AM Factor</u>
5 Powerful Tools for
Self-Discovery

To: Robert
Stay faithful

Andy D. Smith

ISBN-13: 978-1539007470

ISBN-10: 1539007472

TABLE OF CONTENTS

DEDICATION

To The Almighty God

I want to thank God for stretching me beyond my scope of comprehension. He is the reason why I am who I am today. I thank Him for the Wisdom and Understanding He released into my heart to make this dream a reality.

To Every Dreamer and Vision Carrier

This book is dedicated to you. You are the inspiration behind this journey and I hope after walking through this amazing process you come out with an unquenchable fire to climb the ladder of success without fail. It is time for you to Live your Dreams!

To My Supporters and Partners

I want to thank you for your consistent support of what I've been assigned to accomplish on the earth. When I win, we all win. Our desire is to simply change lives one person at a time. I am grateful for every encouraging word spoken in my life, as well as every negative word because they both have been very instrumental in allowing me to become the man I am today.

ACKNOWLEDEMENTS

I would like to personally thank all of the people who have been instrumental in my life over the years. I would not be who I am today if it wasn't for you. I am grateful for your support and prayers. It is because of you this moment is a reality!

To My Family

Thank you for always having my back and holding me accountable to be the best that I can be. The success I will encounter will be a strong representation of what's been instilled in me from you all! Thank you again for always believing in me.

To My Friends/Church Family

This has been one of the most amazing seasons of my life and because of you I have learned so much about myself. This book is a sincere testimony of lessons learned through our relationships. I really appreciate all you have been to me and I declare that "The Best Is Yet To Come For Us."

PREFACE

The book you are about to read is not just any ordinary book. Through this project I have watched my mindset and life change in exponential ways. *This book has been designed with your Self-Discovery in mind.* Are you tired of living beneath your God-given potential? Well, it's time that you do something about it. It's time for you to go after your dreams! We both know you were created to be successful in this life but sometimes we need that extra push. Reader, I'm about to push you!

Within the pages of this book, you will notice that as you read, I will be talking to you through you. It was intentionally and strategically ordered so that *you* can encourage *you*. As you read, allow these words that you will speak over yourself to take a grip of your heart and spirit. Assuredly, you will watch the sure results of Success and Self-Discovery become second nature to you. Are you ready to see what happens when your heart, mind, and spirit align together with one purpose?

You are definitely at the edge of something so big that it will literally defy all human logic. I'm glad to be a part of your next level. Success is knocking at your door. It is time for you to find out who you really are! You've waited for this moment, so let's go! I'm Ready!

-Andy

THE INTRODUCTION

Success - the way of life that everybody wants to partake in. *Two questions remain, what does it take to be successful in life? Secondly, how do I discover the hidden potential on the inside of me?* There are a ton of avenues that can lead you to success, but there is only one person who can stop you from attaining that place of success -you! you are the determining factor in how far you go in life. Everybody has the desire to be somebody in this world, the next question is "How Bad Do You Want It"? How bad do you want to see yourself in a new way of life? The decision is solely up to you.

Defeat is not an option to a person who desires to be successful. It doesn't matter how many people reject you or say no to your dream, there is something that's been programmed on the inside of you called, Try Again! Refuse to take no for an answer! The life you want to create for you and your family all depends on the work ethic and drive you possess as a person. you can either live a mediocre life or go for ultimate wealth. The choice is yours!

As we attempt to uncover and discover all that God has placed on the inside of you, please know that this journey has one audience and that's YOU! You are the person who has the key to your potential. You are the person who has been equipped with multiple talents, so it's your job as you read this book to locate everything that's been placed on the inside of you. This journey to Self-Discovery will assuredly create a life and path for you that has never been trailed. So, put your thinking cap on...it's time to find out who you really are!

The I Am Factor will serve as a practical but realistic guide to help you understand not only the mindset of a successful person but it will also prepare you for day to day challenges that occur on the road to Self-Discovery. Faith and Confidence are vital keys to your success. Make a decision to allow nothing to stop you from seeing your dream become a reality. This book will encourage you as well as convict you in the areas you may need strengthening.

I encourage you to block out all outside distractions and allow these moments of self-evaluation to serve as a surgical tool removing any doubt you may have concerning who you were created to be. You were created to win. Your faith in you will help you overcome any hurdle on this journey. Your faith will be shaken of course, but whatever the situation it will only serve as a lesson. You will come out with Victory.

CHAPTER ONE
I AM MY FIRST AUDIENCE
The Real Me

First Things First

Before I begin this journey to freedom let me be honest with myself. I know I'm not the only one who has made mistakes. The truth of the matter is I am the only one responsible that has to take full responsibility for my mistakes. I am admitting at this moment that I am not perfect but I am chosen. I have been in some very compromising positions in my life and honestly I know it was nobody but God who helped me make it out. I am sure I may just actually mess up again but the difference is I will be more alert to the environments and relationships I allow myself to be in. I am ready to experience my better days. So I am making the conscious decision not to only think better but do better.

I AM READY FOR MY LIFE TO CHANGE!

The Power of Repentance

As I begin this life-changing encounter it is vitally important that I understand the power of the reset button. God has promised me life and wholeness according to (John 10:10). I am now in the perfect position to reestablish my love and passion for my assignment. But first, I must make the conscious decision to allow Jesus to be the Lord of my life and my call. (1 Corinthians 6:20) I am no longer my own. The price that was paid for me can never be repaid, but because I now understand the importance of sacrifice, I today pledge to give God my heart, my life, my plans, and my dreams.

MY PRAYER

Today, I repent for anything that has caused me to be inconsistent in my walk with Christ. I denounce any hindrances, blockages and distractions that are trying to interfere with the purpose and plan of God for my life. I confess my faults and shortcomings to a risen King. I accept you Jesus as the Lord of My life. I choose today to walk and live for you. I choose to trust your plan for my life. I thank you that I am now FORGIVEN! My past has been erased in you! I AM NEW!   In Jesus Name, Amen.

My Declaration

I declare that my life will never be the same after this moment. I declare that I shall walk in the newness of life. I declare that my purpose shall be fulfilled and God shall use my life as a testimony of Redemption and Grace. I declare that I am a winner in Christ and the Victory over failure has already been won. My life belongs to God.

THE TRUTH

Okay, I have started this new journey, where do I go from here? I don't even know my purpose in life? I have been told so many negative things in my life, I'm having a hard time even believing that I can engage success. I was told that I would never be anything. I was told that I was a mistake and that I wasn't even supposed to be here. How do I silence the emotions and statements of failure that I've watched even the generations before me struggle with? I just don't understand how one person can take so much. But, since I understand this is my responsibility, I am going to end this pity party and get up from here. I am going to do what I should've done a long time ago - THINK DIFFERENTLY! I am going to start speaking my end from the beginning. I am going to speak life to myself. **I Am ready to find out who I really am!**

UNDERSTANDING WHO, I AM

Who Am I?

Since I have now given my life back to Jesus Christ and my assignment, I now need to begin engaging my purpose and destiny head on. I have been chosen for such a time as this. (Ester 4:14) The enemy doesn't care about me going to worship services weekly. The enemy only gets fearful when I finally realize who God has called me to be. The Word of God is my manual for success. When I begin to walk fully in my purpose, there is nothing or no good thing God will withhold from me if I walk upright before Him. I understand my destiny is aligned with God's original plan for my life. So it is my choice to walk in His will and not my own. God has shown me who I am in Him so I choose to agree with God.

My Prayer

Father, I thank you for revealing to me who I am in you. I understand my strength and purpose lies within your will. Today I accept my new identity in you. It's by the Grace of God I am who I am. I thank you for shining the light of your word on every negative word spoken over my life by others and myself. I thank you God that I am no longer the same and that my new life shall testify of my relationship with you. In Jesus Name, Amen!

My Declaration

I declare today that I am walking in my true identity. I declare that I am free of the spirit of fear. I declare I do not possess the spirit of fear but power, love, and a sound mind. I declare that today I shall only speak over my life what the Word of God says about me. I am the blessed and favored of God. I declare I know who I am. I AM FREE FROM FEAR.

THE TRUTH

Okay, here comes the hard part. I knew it was coming. I knew the time would come where the process would begin. So I am at a point in my life where I have accepted responsibility for my choices in life whether caused by others or self-inflicted. I now know where I stand and I am ready for this to turn around. What is the challenge that's caused me the most conflict? It has to be the way I think. How am I seeing this situation? How am allowing this to affect my day to day life? As of this moment I will no longer think below success and progress. I am changing my life one day at a time by starting with my mind. I was put on earth to make and impact and I will do just that. I am blocking out all negativity that may cause me to second guess my ability to win. If I think like a Champion nothing can stop me from becoming a Champion! **I am changing the way I live by changing the way I think.**

The Change of Mind: I am what I Think

Is it true that I am what I think? Certainly it is. My mind is the place where my image is created. My mind is the place where my future is created. My mind is the place where my dreams and faith collide. But the interesting part is, I'm not even supposed to use my mind according to (Philippians 2:5). So even on my strongest mentally stable day, my mind is useless. I am giving up my mind for the mind of Christ. I am choosing to think on purpose with purpose. My mindset has changed and I now have the Jesus mind. So I now think the way He does.

My Prayer

Father, I thank you for choosing me to do the work of the Kingdom. I humbly submit to you my mind and I thank you for giving me the mind of your son. I thank you that I am no longer seeing things the same. I thank you for working in me the will and do of your good pleasure. I bind all evil thoughts, misunderstandings, and immature perceptions. I step into this new season with a new thirst, a new hunger, and most of all A NEW MIND! In Jesus Name, Amen!

My Declaration

I declare that I have the mind of Christ. I declare that I only think thoughts that are pure, true, and of a good report. I declare that Jeremiah 29:11 shall be my daily bread. I declare that no enemy shall gain any power over my mind. I declare that my mind is alert and that my spiritual discernment shall work hand in hand for the protection of my future. I declare that I will only produce mature and clear perceptions. I declare that I shall live a life of Focus and Favor.

THE TRUTH

I am understanding now that my success is not predicated upon who likes me or puts my name in the wind. I am the key to my future. I am the key to my success. I am the key to unlocking an eternal legacy. If I don't believe in my dream, why should I expect anybody else to do so? My attitude towards success is the determining factor in how far I will go. The negative words and fears that try to attack my future only have power if I allow them to register in my mind and spirit. But because I have a new attitude towards my success, I will make sure I remain positive at all times.

MY ATTITUDE TOWARDS SUCCESS WILL
ALWAYS REMAIN POSTIVE!

MY ATTITUDE TOWARDS SUCCESS

I See Greater for my Life

I have learned the secret to overcoming negativity when it comes to my future. I am the only one responsible for my success. I refuse to walk around in fear of what I may not understand, but trusting and believing that God has the final say so. My future has already been planned by God and all I have to is come into alignment with His plan and allow Him to lead and guide me. The things I see for my life no one may understand, but I know that the ultimate destination is Success!

My Prayer

Father, I thank you for working on my attitude and vision. I may not understand everything you're doing in this season but I'm smart enough to know that you know what's best for me. So I ask that you continue to teach me how to trust you even when I don't know what's going on. I have faith that supersedes any doubt. I now choose to see what you see and say what you say. I agree with your plan for my life. In Jesus Name, Amen.

My Declaration

I declare that my attitude has shifted to one of a positive outlook. My attitude shall be a reflection of the true intents of my heart. I declare that success is my portion and failure is not an option. I declare that even in the rough times I will not give up, back down, or throw in the towel! I declare success is my ultimate destination. I declare that my mind has already traveled to where God is leading me, so now I declare the manifestation of His plans for me!

THE TRUTH

I have been taught how to have faith in the things I want to accomplish in life. I was also taught one valuable lesson that I must believe in me. Me having faith in what God will do and me having faith in myself are two totally different things. I am now learning to encourage myself daily. If nobody else believes in me, it does not matter why...because I believe in me. I believe that all things are possible. There is no level of success I can't conquer. I am my faith! I only speak words of freedom and progress over my life. I strengthen my belief factor by consistently saying what I want to see in my life. I believe that I shall experience the greatest era of my life. I believe that what I carry cannot be duplicated because I am an original.

I BELIEVE ALL THINGS ARE POSSIBLE!

I BELIEVE IN ME: It's Going To Happen

I've been feeling this thing pushing me for a while now. I couldn't really put my hands on it, but it's a force I've never experienced before. It took me a while to understand why I started seeing things differently and responding in an unusual way. But whatever is was, started to cause things to align in such a way that every time it happens, I started feeling more powerful. And then it happened, it all became clear...I got the answer to my questions! I STARTED TO BELIEVE IN MYSELF. What an amazing feeling to wake up knowing that any day now you're going to be on top of the world. I believe in what God has invested in me and there is nothing that can shake my belief.

My Prayer

Father, I thank you for placing a fire down on the inside of me that cannot be quenched. I thank you for teaching me how to trust you through it all. I thank you for establishing a level of Faith in me that lets me know that I cannot lose with you on my side. I thank you that not only do I believe I can do all things through you, I know I will accomplish everything you've invested in my heart. I will die empty. In Jesus Name, Amen.

My Declaration

I declare that I won't stop believing in myself. I declare that I have everything I need to succeed on the inside of me. I declare that every place I connect to my faith and belief in the supernatural has already gone before me. I declare that I will stand tall in the faith that growing daily on the inside of me. I see where I want to be, and I believe I am on my way to a place of prosperity and wealth. I declare that I AM UNSTOPPABLE! I declare that this is the day I dreamed about. I declare I am here and I will enjoy this place because it was my belief that got me here.

THE TRUTH

Today is a very interesting day. I don't know why I figured it wasn't going to happen. Why would I even try to make myself believe that I wasn't going to see today? It's been a long journey, and it's not been as easy others have made it out to be. I am feeling all types of emotions right now and it's still early in the game. But I can't help but to be excited because I have been assured of Victory. you know what that means right? Yep! - you got it...YOU WIN! You mean I have the power to declare the end from the beginning...OF COURSE I DO! Man, you are talking about some good news, I was a little worried for minute there, things were looking a bit funny. But hey, I'm good now! What was I even worried about, this was won from the very start. I got victory which means, everybody connected to me wins!

I HAVE THE POWER TO DECLARE THE
END FROM THE BEGINNING!

My Victory is Sure: It's Taken Care Of

I was concerned about how it was going to happen, not only how but when. I know I was told to just trust and believe and know that in due time things would come together, but I just wanted to see some manifestation you know with my physical eye. I believe this happened for a reason, if I didn't have this challenge there would be no way I could increase in faith. If everything was handed to me on a silver platter I wouldn't appreciate it. But why did I ever stop believing that my victory was being threatened? My victory is sure and I already know that this fight is fixed, they don't know that but I do! Let's get it together okay? The way has already been made.

My Prayer

Father, I thank you for encouraging my heart and having my back. I don't know why I doubted you in the first place? you haven't lost a battle yet so why would you start now? I've never not seen you some through, so I don't know where that came from, but we are good now. I just needed a little boost and you did that. you are dependable and I never have to worry about you being who you told me you would be. Thanks for taken care of this before it even started. In Jesus Name, Amen.

My Declaration

I declare that I am walking in not only Total Victory but Uncommon Victory. I declare that my battles are won before they even begin. I declare that angels are consistently going before me making all of the crooked paths straight. I declare that Victorious is my name. I declare that I walk in boldness coupled with humility and discernment I declare that I will fulfill my purpose with power and persistence. I declare that I walk in SURE VICTORY!

NOTES TO SELF

_____

_____

_____

_____

_____

_____

_____

_____

_____

_____

_____

_____

_____

_____

_____

A Personal Note From Andy

Through my life experiences one valuable lesson that I have learned Is to always understand that I am my first audience. I will only release to the public what I practice in private. There are many people who claim to want success, but never take the time to get to know themselves. As you grow in your endeavor to be successful in life it's vital that you understand the importance of originality and self-discipline. There will never be a person who will be able to format and outline your dream like you.

It's very easy to talk about what you want to do in life, but it's another thing to buckle down and do it. I use to tell people all the time that I was going to be the greatest organist of all time-and it sounded really good. But there was one problem, because of my gifted skill-set, I completely stop practicing. I totally stopped investing the necessary time it took to become great. So once laziness became a pattern and habitual ritual it ultimately caused me to settle for being content. Self-Discipline is very important when it comes to discovering hidden potential.

You must begin to challenge yourself daily to go beyond your comfortable place. There is a popular vernacular that says "anything worth having is worth fighting for." And in this case, you may have to fight you to help you. Your first step is to attempt to gain an understanding of what you're carrying on the inside. You were created with purpose in mind, so when you fail to achieve your purpose, it is evident that something is missing. The good news is "there is no expiration date on your purpose!"

I encourage you as you continue this journey of discovering who you are, to approach each day with a mindset that says, I will not allow myself to settle for this place. I had to literally become fed up with living pay check to paycheck. It doesn't matter if you have to talk out loud to yourself, but encourage yourself that you can do it.

Your attitude towards self-discovery will determine how you proceed in life. What you fail to reveal, you cannot kill.

There are something's on the inside of you that can make this journey pleasant or painful. If nobody else believes in what you have, you believe in you. It doesn't take everybody to like you, just that one person who has been assigned to change your life forever. Because I was willing to stop and begin to deal with me, I was able to discover talents I didn't even know I had.

I didn't know that I had a winning personality and was able to change a person's entire day by making them laugh. So, now when I come into any room, it is expected of me to lighten up the room with laughter. I only saw a musician on the inside, but because I never stopped looking for more ways to be a better me, I stumbled upon something great. Today, I am broadening my horizons and entering Christian Comedy.

Remember to always believe in you. This is the season where you have no other option but to succeed, but you must find that one thing that separates you from everybody else and begin to fully develop that gift. You can do it!

CHAPTER TWO
COMMANDING YOUR AUDIENCE

Understanding My Internal Capabilities

I know this may be really weird to me, but it's amazing that the entire earth revolves around this one word...Communication. It is important to me that I understand what I speak creates my tomorrow. As I think back how hard it has been to communicate what I've been seeing in my spirit. I use to think it was impossible to speak things into existence, but it's not. I am excited about my weapon of mass creation≥ I am exchanging fear for faith, and impossible for possible. I control what happens in my life by what I speak into the atmosphere. I choose to speak only positivity into my future and all things are working for my good.

I AM UPGRADING MY COMMUNICATION FROM SPEAKING DOUBT-FILLED WORDS TO SPEAKING FAITH-FILLED WORDS.

UPGRADING MY COMMUNICATION

What I say actually does matter

Have I really taken the time out to examine what I've been speaking over my life? Have my words been the reason why I haven't excelled in certain areas? Have the words I've allowed others to speak over my life been the determining factor in my lack of progress? Well, if any of those denominators are true, they because ineffective as of this moment. I am now becoming more alert to what's being spoken over and into my life. I was created to win and every statement being released over my future shall be aligned with that concept.

My Prayer

Father, I thank you for teaching me the right words to speak over my life. I will only say what you have already spoken over my life from the foundations of the world. I trust your plans more than my own. I thank you for faith-filled words being my daily portion. I pray to continue to always be sensitive to my communication and what's being released from my mouth. In Jesus Name, Amen

My Declaration

I declare that I am upgrading my communication to only faith-filled words. I declare that no negativity concerning me or anyone else shall depart my lips. I declare that my words are creating a better tomorrow for me and those that are connected to me. I declare that a successful future is my pre-destined destination, and every word I speak is only being used to bring it closer to a reality.

THE TRUTH

What is the use of me having a dream that I want to fulfill and I don't believe I can? If anybody is going to believe in what I have to offer I must first believe in me. I can't allow circumstances and situations to dictate and detour my faith in me. My faith is all I have. It's my personal support system that's invisible to the natural eye at times but strong enough to be acted on. I have the faith I need to see this vision through and as long as I keep believing it will come to pass. I don't pick up my faith one day and put it down or only refer to it when things are good. My faith is the vehicle that will transport from my NOW to my NEXT.

MY FAITH IN ACTION IS ALL IT TAKES TO SEE THIS THROUGH!

THE FAITH WALK: I CAN SEE IT!

I can see it! I can sense it! I can almost taste it! What am I am talking about? I'm talking about my freedom! I am using an extreme level of faith in this season and it's working. My faith literally has me believing for things I know I cannot do it the natural. I literally see it happening before my very eyes. I'm so encouraged right now! I am right at the brink of something so big that it's going to blow the minds of everyone around me. Well, from the looks of it...it's going to blow my mind as well! So here I go, my next season has arrived and I'm more ready for it than it is for me. My Faith Got Me Here!

My Prayer

Father, without faith it is impossible to please you. So today I place my faith not in myself but in the One who holds tomorrow. What you're doing in my life and the doors you're opening for me are nothing short of miracles. I have the sense enough to understand to know that I can't do this without you. So I trust you with my life, my plans, and my future. I'm stretching myself on this particular assignment but because my faith is not in myself or man but in you, I know that this shall be the greatest season of my life. In Jesus Name, Amen

My Declaration

I declare that the Faith I have is unshakeable, unwavering, and undisturbed. I declare that I shall stand in the midst of adversities because of Strong Faith. I declare that my faith is becoming contagious to those that are around me. I declare that I carry a faith that activates the supernatural in my life and causes other to wonder who is the source of my success. I declare that my faith is being elevated to a new dimension. I declare that my faith is all I need and it shall speak for itself.

THE TRUTH

My dream was given to me, but I also know I can't accomplish it by myself. It's too big for me. It's more than the human mind can comprehend. I have to surround myself with people who see what I see. I see things differently and it's important that I associate with people with either like faith or greater faith. I see something so big, that it could very well defy human logic. I am becoming very careful about who I surround myself with. I want to be able to know who's in my corner and who's not. I am not bias but I am cautious.

I am in a new place and my associations have to align with my new season.

I CAN'T CONNECT TO EVERYBODY

THE SUPPORT SYSTEM

Who Am I Dealing With?

What do I see when I look inside of my circle of influence? Who are the speaking that are speaking the same words of Faith that I am? Who do I acknowledge as my sphere of counsel? These are questions I have to ask because where I am going I won't have room for unnecessary error. I am applying a greater level of wisdom to my decisions and relationships. I have a world to conquer and a God to glorify. I am grateful for those people who serve as my check and balance. I have an amazing support system. A set of people who are not intimidated by my success. An effective Support System will not only stand with you during the mountaintop experience but as well in the dark valley experiences as well.

My Prayer

Father, I thank you for placing real people in my life. I thank you thank you are giving me daily wisdom on how to handle my affairs with Integrity. I thank you that I am never alone and because of you I have everything I need. I thank you for aligning my relationships with your plan for my life. you are such an amazing God that you will not allow me to be deceived or caught off guard by any secret agent that comes for my demise. I thank you God for your divine protection that surrounds me like a shield. In Jesus Name, Amen.

My Declaration

I declare that I am surrounded by a Support System that only wants the best for my life. I declare that every one that's connected to me shall benefit in some way or another from this amazing season. I declare that my relationships are nothing less than God-ordained and Purpose-driven. I declare that I am surrounded by God-fearing people who love me unconditionally. I declare that I am about to meet people who have waiting to invest into my dreams!

THE TRUTH

I know I can be stubborn at times. I've been known to like things just one way and that's my way. But I am learning on this journey to success that I don't have all the answers and my way is not the only way. I want to be successful in every area of my life and that sometimes comes with learning new things. I refuse to be a person of limited knowledge. With the assignment I have, I have to be able to learn from others that have already traveled this road. I understand that there are always multiple ways to get a job done. I am not putting this many hours of work to get to a successful career to just mess it all because I refuse to listen. It is okay for me to trust proven advice. I will be even more successful if I learn to be flexible.

I KNOW HOW TO TAKE PROVEN ADVICE.

IT CAN'T ALWAYS BE MY WAY

I Am Flexible And Open-Minded

When it comes to my future I only want things done my way. It's my career and my life so it needs to be done my way. It is this type of thinking that will keep me living one-dimensional. I have more to offer than just a point of view. I have ideas on the inside of me that are capable of revolutionizing human logic. My only concern is me only listening to others about me when it comes to me. But I am pretty sure that where I am someone has already been so this is no new territory.

So, I will adjust and be cooperative when it comes to others helping me get to where I'm trying to go.

My Prayer

Father, help me not to only lean on my knowledge concerning my future. I know you are placing people in my paths with good intentions and pure motives. I ask that you help settle my heart when it comes to trusting people and not allow me to run off the help that you are sending. I thank you that I am learning even now how to trust you even when I can't trace you. But because I know you love me, and you only want me to prosper, I'll do whatever I need to do to ensure that I live out my full potential in you. In Jesus Name, Amen.

My Declaration

I declare that today is the day I learn how to listen to proven advice. I declare that I will not become boastful and arrogant as if my way is the only way. I declare that I will make sound decisions concerning my career and future. I declare that I am walking in wisdom every day. I declare that even when I don't understand what's going on, I will trust the plan of God. I declare that my future is bright and I have people already assigned on this journey to help me. I declare that I am Flexible and Open-Minded to new ideas, patterns, and avenues of success.

No matter how excited I get about being successful there is one thing that levels me every time no matter how high I am. I have learned that they are the true people who inspire success and tenacity in me. These people are able to reach my heart when no one else can. I have learned never to discount them or discredit them because after all the lights are off and the cameras are gone, they will be there with me and for me. I wasn't able to handpick them but I will not trade them for nothing in the world. I need them probably more than they need me sometimes. I cherish my relationships and I definitely cherish the people God created in my bloodline. I stand for My Family. I need My Family. My Family needs me.

MY FAMILY INSPIRES ME TO ACHIEVE GREATER.

FAMILY MATTERS

Unconditional Love

What am I feeling right now? I love these people! I am abundantly blessed and I want to make sure they know it. I won't be the one to rise to fame and forget about my family. They may not be able to go with me to the top, but one thing is for sure I will always acknowledge them for what they have instilled in me. I will always try to live as an example of integrity to them so that it will inspire them to live their dreams. I have experienced unconditional love in many ways and my family has been one of the leading forces. So, I can't leave them behind. I cannot live as if they don't exist. I am not going to forfeit my future because of them but I will fight to awakened the fire of success within them every chance I get.

My Prayer

Father, I thank you for my family. I thank you that you entrusted them to me and entrusted me to them. I don't have a perfect family but who does? I thank you that you do all things well and you have chosen me a light to my family as well as a testament. I thank you that my family is covered in your love and that you have a plan for them as well. I ask that you continue to keep your arms around us. Family was your first institution and I vow to always keep it as my top priority. In Jesus Name, Amen.

My Declaration

I declare that my family is the blessed of God. I declare that my Family shall live out their full potential. I declare that I will fight to show my Family a better way of living. I declare that I shall be the Joseph of my Family. I declare that unity and love hold my family together. I declare that I shall serve as a tool of mending for broken families around the world. I declare that Family is God's first institution and I will teach this principle everywhere I go. I declare that Family Love is Unconditional Love.

THE TRUTH

It is one thing for me to hear how successful and blessed I'm going to be, but it's a totally different challenge when I come face to face with that opportunity. People have tried to prepare me for this moment in time, but I never knew it would be so scary. It's not a fear that says I can't do it, it's a fear that says...you're here already? Where did the time go? I guess while I was focusing on other people my opportunity was coming at an alarming speed that I didn't expect. But now that I'm here, the doors of success have been opened to me...what do I do? What do I do to make sure that I seized the moment God created for me? Where do I go from here?

THE OPPORTUNITY OF A LIFETIME IS STARRING ME IN MY FACE - WHAT IS MY NEXT STEP?

FACE TO FACE WITH MY FUTURE

I'm looking Success in the Face

I am now forced to look my promise in the face, but why do I feel this way? I know it's supposed to be exciting that I'm finally getting to live my dream, and everything I've prayed for is becoming a reality - but am I ready? I see such a bright future ahead for me and I'm standing face to face with my purpose. It's finally here! My time has come to show the world what has been invested in me...but wait...what do I do? What do I say? When do I move? I do it all NOW! I am at the crossroads of success and my prayers have been answered. So I will not run away from my future...I will run directly into it with tenacity.

My Prayer

Father, thank you for opening my eyes to know where I stand when it comes to my Destiny. I thank you that I could have missed this moment by worrying and concerning myself with stuff beyond my control. It's been quite a journey and I could have quit! But you have given me grace to endure and now that I'm here, I plan to enjoy the season you have brought me to! In Jesus Name, Amen.

My Declaration

I declare that I will not become fearful of the unknown. I declare that I deserve to be here and nothing will stop me from enjoying this season of my life. I declare that what's to come will be better than what's been. I declare that I shall gain even more momentum now that I'm where I am supposed to be. I am standing at the door of my future so what do I do? I WALK IN! It's My Time To Shine!

NOTES TO SELF

A Personal Note From Andy

The chapter that you just read, brought back so many memories in my personal life. People who know me know I love to talk. There were times when I had no idea what was being discussed but because I love to talk, I had to release my 2 cents. Communication for me became second nature because of my field. But I began to see certain characteristics that were not becoming of a person who was on his way to being a success. I found myself a lot of times doing a lot of talking but saying nothing.

What you must understand about communication is, if you're not going to speak positive end results of any situation you may end up in, it's best that you remain silent. Whether you believe it or not, your words do have power, and you will be held responsible for what you speak into the atmosphere. I have now become more careful about who I allow to speak into my life.

Words that go into the atmosphere have the power to produce desired results. I had to personally begin being more careful about what I was saying over my own life. There are times where situations don't look like what God showed you, and it gives the enemy pleasure to hear you speak negativity over your situation. But here's a way to confuse even those who are doubters: "Say what you see, until you begin to see what you said."

Be careful of what you allow in your ears and your spirit. You have the ability to condition your spirit to only receive words of faith and positivity.

It's easy to have people in your corner that always agree with you, but what about when you're wrong? I had to understand that I couldn't always have my way. There were some decisions that needed to be made that I wasn't able to make alone. I encourage you no matter what you have set up concerning your success, there is nothing more important than a powerful and stabilized support system. They can sometimes see things in you that you are not able to see. Sometimes, it's okay to trust people, especially when they have proven that they have your best interest at heart.

The time is coming when you will have to call things for what they are. Now is the time where your rubber has met the road and you have to stand accountable for the things you have said. Now that you are standing face to face with your future, you have to be very careful in the decisions that you make as well as the decisions you fail to make. Are you ready to move forward? Are you ready to experience the life that many only dream about? I dare you to speak the end result from the beginning!

CHAPTER THREE
EXPOSURE BRINGS FREEDOM
Being True To Myself

THE TRUTH

I had to question myself and ask am I afraid of what my life will turn out to be. Why was I afraid? Why am I afraid? What do I have to do to not be scared anymore? It simple. FACE IT! I decided that I was going to face the thing I was afraid of. I told myself I couldn't do it, so when others said it, it made it easier to believe. I don't have to be afraid of my future. I can even go to say I don't have to be afraid of my present. It may not be those, am I afraid that my past will come back to haunt me? – Geesh!

I WILL NOT BE AFRAID OF MY PAST,
PRESENT, OR FUTURE.

FACING MY FEARS

I'm not Giving in!

I am in a place now where certain decisions are not as hard to make as they use to be. It is one thing to know where you are supposed to be in life and not want it, but it's another thing to be afforded the opportunity and be afraid of it. I am no longer allowing my fears to keep me from my future. I was created to be great and nothing or no' one can stop that but me. I now understand fear and faith cannot occupy the same house! I am going after my dreams! I refuse to lose and I will not allow fear to cause me to miss out on the biggest opportunity of my life. I stand in the face of fear and say YOU LOSE.

My Prayer

Father, I thank you that you have given me the power to denounce all my fears. I thank you that nothing I've done is worth forfeiting my future over. I thank you for the opportunity to live my best life now. I understand now that my faith is the strongest force I have. I now exercise the authority that you've given me and I take my rightful place as Kingdom Ambassador. I activate my faith and speak only that which you have said about me. I am free! In Jesus Name, Amen.

My Declaration

I declare that today is the last time I will battle with Fear. I declare that my mind is free and my spirit is open to see the goodness that God has planned for me. I declare that I will walk in Supernatural Faith and Unexplainable Favor. I declare Fear no longer has a hold on my heart and mind. I am free from the fear of failure, fear of my past and future. I declare that my faith shall stand tall. I declare that this day shall be written in history as the day I won.

THE TRUTH

I never understood how change could be so amazing but difficult at the same time. I thought going through a change would just be some light thing that I could adjust to and keep moving. But this is where I found the problem, when things change beyond my control. I would at least like to have a say so in what is taking place in my life. When change takes place I'm usually never prepared for it. But because it's necessary and often times unavoidable I have learned to adjust. Fighting change is fighting my future. I can't fight my own success so I will just allow change to come and complete it's intended assignment.

CHANGE NEVER GIVES YOU A FORMAL NOTICE OF ARRIVAL.

THE TRUTH ABOUT CHANGE

This Is For My Good

I can always expect for something unusual to happen without my permission. I know there are things I have control of but there also things I don't.

The truth is, change for me isn't always good neither is it always welcomed. But one thing I have learned that every time I resist change, it only makes the process harder. Change comes in for two reason to realign and redirect. I enjoy always being in the know until change comes along and shows me that I'm not as powerful as I think. But there is one thing for sure, change has always and will continue to expose where I am in my process. How I respond to change determines how I respond to elevation.

My Prayer

Father, thank you for allowing me to experience the different diversities of life. I know you control all things and nothing enters my life or exits my life without your permission. I thank you for not only allowing things to come and change my environment, but also my mindset. The way I think now has been a determining factor in my progress. you control change, as a matter of fact you are Change. you rule the world and every season moves by your command, so I know I'm in good hands. Thank you God for changing me! In Jesus Name, Amen.

My Declaration

I declare that I will not resist the Power of Change. I declare that every change that takes place in my life is working for my good. I declare that I'm changing for the better and the change I needed has already started. I declare that as I change, every person that's connected to me will benefit from the change. I declare that all change is not bad and that this change is working for my good.

THE TRUTH

As I sit here thinking about all of the things I've been through in my life, it baffles me on how I actually survived it. People will never know how many tears I've shared to get to this point. People look at me smiling on certain days and they have the slightest idea that I had to literally force myself to do it. I know it takes pain to push us into greatness sometimes but sometimes I wonder why me? I have never met a person who just loved to experience pain, and when I do I'm running! But I have come to realize that what I have went through has made me the person I am today. I am learning to take all of the pain and rejoice because I know it's working for my good. I may not like how it makes me feels but I will certainly endure because on the other side on my pain is peace!

MY PAIN IS WORKING FOR MY GOOD!

MY PAIN HAS PURPOSE

Why Me?

I've always wondered how situations that are meant to take me out end up working for my good? I never know when God is designing or orchestrating a situation to teach me a lesson. So I've learned to always keep a positive attitude about what I go through. I will not allow situations to get into my spirit and allow me to become bitter. I know that everything I will go through will work for my good. My Pain has Purpose. The Purpose of my Pain is to give me a clearer perspective on life and my future. I don't run from my circumstances, I look them in the eye and tell them I'm ready. I am built to survive storms. I'm an eagle, when the storms get tough, I simply soar above the storm.

My Prayer

Father, I know you are working something special in my life and that's why you are taking me through these series of trials. I thank you because I understand that you know what's best for me. I thank you because you know exactly what I'm made of and how much I can handle. I thank you for every painful encounter I've had, every tear I've shed, and every lost I've had to endure. But today is a new day and I now know how to counter-attack my pain, and I do that with joy! In Jesus Name, Amen.

My Declaration

I declare that I shall never bow down to the attacks sent against me. I declare that I have a new outlook on the challenges that I face on a day to day basis. I declare that I was created to conquer and subdue. I declare that my pain will not cause me to forfeit my future. I declare that I am stronger than I've ever been. I declare that I am a Winner. I declare that my painful experiences are working for me and making me a better person. I declare that I've Positioned for Power!

THE TRUTH

In order for me to embrace this new season of my life, it is imperative that I realize that I am no longer under the bondage of yesterday. I am not the same person I use to be. I saw my change taking place long before it happens. I know that I am definitely where I want to be, but I'm certainly not where I was. I am a different person. I know it was intended for my past to hold me captive, but I got free! This will not be the only day I am forced to remember what I use to be or what I use to do. I am not looking into who I was to try to find out who I will become. I am a new creation set on the earth for a purpose that has never been fulfilled. I am excited about my future. My past is not being considered in this season when it comes to level of my success. I'm going as high and as far as I want to.

I AM NOT WHO I USE TO BE.

YESTERDAY IS GONE: I'm not the same!

There will always be cases where someone will walk up and say "I remember when". I am not going to allow the past failures of my life to determine the level of greatness I achieve. I am not the same person I was before this change took place. I am a new creation. Everything about me is new! The way I think, the way I live, the way I believe, and the way I achieve have all become new. I have a new mind and a new way of doing things. Yesterday is time that cannot be fixed, only remembered. I choose not to dwell on what happened or what didn't happen. My future is predicated solely upon what I do now. I am free from the spirit of yesterday and I am moving forward.

My Prayer

Father, I thank you for closing the door to my past. I know I made a lot mistakes, bad decisions, and used poor judgment. But you have helped me to better every area of my life. I have experienced so my joy and peace in this season and it's all because I no longer look at yesterday as a crutch, but as a stepping stone. I thank you that my past is just that, my past. It's Over! I am grateful that you allowed me to go through what I went through. I thank you for My Freedom!

In Jesus Name, Amen.

My Declaration

I declare that I am free from my past. I declare that I am no longer bound by yesterday. I declare that everything I have encountered is working on my behalf. I declare that all relationships from my past that are non-beneficial are left in my yesterday. I declare that I will embrace my future and appreciate every opportunity given for me to succeed in life. I declare that today is a new day and yesterday will be no more.

THE TRUTH

I use to think the only thing it took to succeed was Belief and Faith. I was sadly mistaken. There is a force that is greater than any other force in my life now that consistently keeps me shooting for greater. I have not only built up my faith for this season but I have gained a greater love for what I am called to do. I love the gifts God have given me. I have learned to embrace the assignment with joy and not sadness. The love I have for my success and what I carry has been very essential to my process. I am focused because I love what I do. I am making exponential leaps of faith because I love what I do. I have seen unexplainable results because I love what I do.

MY SUCCESS IS APART OF MY HEART

WHERE IS YOUR HEART?

A Love that can't be denied

There are times when I wanted to give up on my call and try something different. If I can be honest with myself, I still am not able to effectively articulate how I got here. But now that I'm here, I wouldn't trade it for nothing in the world. I didn't just wake up saying I love my assignment. It takes a steadfast love to conquer the fear of failing. My heart speaks to me in the stillness of the night and reminds me how grateful I am to be considered a voice of influence in the earth. When I fell in love with who and what I was called to be, it made becoming and doing it more exciting. I am overwhelmingly in love with who I have become, not as a sense of pride, but more so a sense of feeling accomplished.

My Prayer

Father, I thank you teaching me how to love me, and even more so who you have called me to be. I thank you thank I no longer look at my assignment in the earth as a hard task but now as a privilege. I have grown to love my call and in doing that I have grown to love me. I thank you that you loved me past my faults and failures and assured me I could experience life abundantly. I promise to share this love with all of mankind. Thank you God for showing me an example of true love.

In Jesus Name, Amen.

My Declaration

I declare that I shall always be grateful for my assignment. I declare that I am loving the person I am becoming. I declare that I do my assignment in the earth with joy and passion. I declare that I will never see myself as just an ordinary person. I declare that my heart is connected to my assignment and I will love my journey to success as much as I love me. I declare that I will teach others the key to my success by loving what you've been called to do.

THE TRUTH

Okay...it's rough out here! I have been through a lot of things since I started this journey towards my success. But I didn't know my skin had to be so tough. I understand that you have to fight for what you want but nobody told me that it's a war zone trying to climb the ladder of success. It would make sense to stop and just quit and let them have it. However, I am not a quitter! I am not a person who throws in the towel at the first sign of resistance. I am going to take a minute and regroup. Yes, I am taking some heavy blows today, if it's not one thing it's another. But the great thing is I am not giving up. I am about to square my shoulders and get back in the ring and fight. I wasn't created to lose. So my lesson today has taught me how string I really am. I refuse to crack under pressure.

I AM GOING TO TAKE A MINUTE AND REGROUP.

ONLY THE STRONG SURVIVE

I Refuse To Crack Under Pressure

It happens to the best of us, and sometimes there is nothing that can be done about it. I've to tell myself that on many occasions recently. I am learning to find inner strength in certain situations, because as much as I want to be successful in life, I now realize that there are something's I have to fight for. I can't be intimidated by those who have already arrived to the place I want to be. I know what I want out of life will not come easy and there will be times when I will have to fight for my success. I am surrounded by many people that desire success and some of them are giving up, but this race is not for people with soft skin. It has been proven on the road to success *"Only The Strong Survive"*.

My Prayer

Father, I didn't know it would get this hard on this road, but you did. you saw this day before it even happened and you knew I would come to you for strength. So, I ask that you give me the wisdom and knowledge on how to handle the tough patches in this journey. I thank you that you are always there when I need you the most. So I am grateful to know I have someone to depend on when I get weak in moments like these. Thank you for encouraging me and renewing my strength for the battle.

In Jesus Name, Amen.

My Declaration

I declare that I am empowered to succeed. I declare that even in the rough patches of live I will not quit. I declare that I shall remain focused and encouraged about my journey. I declare that I am not a quitter. I declare that I shall finish strong. I declare that regardless of the situation or circumstance I will survive each and every trial and come out Victorious. I declare that I am stronger than I've ever been. I declare that I am able to take a licking and keep on ticking. I declare I AM STRENGTH!

NOTES TO SELF

A Personal Note From Andy

Well, I have to be honest, I wasn't looking forward to this particular chapter. Truth be told, no one wants to go back and relive the pains of the past. I had to stop for a minute and just regroup, because I didn't realize how much stuff God spared me through. After struggling with insecurities of my past, I made a decision that I would not live in the past, or in fear of the past anymore. I spent years walking around depressed while still being allowed to minister because of the things I had publicly endured. There were times where I was sure I wasn't going to be able to live those situations down.

I learned the hard way, that when God has a plan for your life, it doesn't matter how hard it gets, there is something on the inside that will not allow you to give up. When you decide to change your ways and align your will with His Will, the journey becomes easier. A lot of people have a problem with change, but change is necessary. Change and exposure reveal two things about you: who you are and where you're going. Everybody wants the lime light, but what happens when that light exposes things about you that you thought were dead?

I had to realize that even though I went through some public exposure, it did not disqualify me from being used by God. My pain and exposure was already counted in the equation. God had to remind me even though I was embarrassed and humiliated, that He was going to use those situations for my good.

So I can, without hesitation say that your pain has purpose. God used my pain in my favor. The process of going through will never be easy, but the reminder of knowing that you are not alone and that you're coming out of it makes it worth it. I no longer live in yesterday. Yesterday no longer controls my tomorrow.

Your past has a way of showing you exactly how much you have matured. I decided to refrain from giving attention to things and people who only remind me of who I use to be. I am not the same person that I once was. I know where my heart is concerning God, and His people. I am no longer allowing yesterday to hinder my current progress. We were created to win. I finally looked within myself and realized that I was my only hindrance.

It doesn't matter how people try to outrun you when it comes to getting their dreams out there. The road to self-discovery is not a competition. There is no special prize for who discovers their gifts and talents first. However, the road to self-discovery can be quite painful and frustrating. They have a saying that "only the strong survive", that's absolutely correct. This journey is about endurance, patience, and consistency. It is vitally important that you master all three.

Being able to endure the attacks, rejections, and unseen occurrences in life play a major role in producing and developing patience. Once your patience has been ignited, you no longer look at situations the same. Patience allows you the opportunity to rest and regroup knowing that this issue is already working in your favor. After patience comes into full play, consistency is the final step. No matter what the problem may be, things of the past or whatever may arise, you must remain focused. I tried it and it worked for me. Don't give in to the pressures and reminders of the past. You are looking at your future right in the face…**GO FOR IT!**

CHAPTER FOUR
THE IMPORTANCE OF
RIGHT CONNECTIONS

*You Will Become
Who You Associate With*

THE TRUTH

It is very easy for me to be caught off guard when I'm focused on being successful. One of the most effective distractions are people. If I could go ahead and be honest about the ordeal, I know I have already encountered both types of people who rule the world today, Beneficial and Non-Beneficial. I know it may seem blunt but it's the truth. I will encounter on the road to fulfilling your purpose people who are able to assist me and those who are not. So let me deal with the non-beneficial people. They are those who seek the majority of my time. Non-beneficial are never sincerely excited about my dreams, but only seek how they can benefit from it. Non-Beneficial people only show me the negatives to your positives, but they are dressed as the voice of reason. Non-Beneficial people will always be connected in some way or the other to the people who are enemies of my success. So be careful of those who talk the right words but say them the wrong way.

I AM KILLING EVERY NON-BENEFICIAL RELATIONSHIP THAT THREATENS THE PROGRESS OF MY FUTURE.

RELATIOSHIPS (NON-BENEFICIAL)

Who are you?

It's been proven over and over again that everybody wants to be a part of something great and successful. I am successful which makes me a target for not only those with good intentions but those not so good. I understand that I am called to do something in the earth that has never been done before, so I am standing alert and cautious of who I allow in my circle. I cannot afford to be tricked, distracted or detoured by people who are not able to finance or enhance my dream.

My Prayer

Father, you know the intents and motives of each person that has or will attempt to connect to me in this new season. I am trusting that you will allow my discernment to become strong enough to make protective decisions against the tricks and plans of the enemy. Thank you for continual wisdom and knowledge concerning unfruitful relationships. I thank you for exposing every assignment that's not pure and that can cause harm to what you've invested in me. In Jesus Name, Amen.

My Declaration

I declare that I shall not walk in deception concerning secrets agents of the enemy. I declare that my mind is alert and my heart is protected. I declare that I shall not retaliate against those who attempt to bring disappointments or snares against me. I declare that every negative influence and hidden trap is being exposed. I declare that I am detached from all non-beneficial relationships.

THE TRUTH

There is a saying that *"Birds of A Feather Flock Together"* - I believe that. I believe I will eventually become what I speak and who or what I associate with. That brings up the second person mentioned in Day Four, The Beneficial Relationship. This type of relationship is full of excitement and extreme possibilities. I need these type of people around me. These are the people who encourage me to shoot beyond the stars. I am surrounding myself with people who understand what it means to be called into Purpose. I am successful so I choose to hang around successful people. I am deciding to live life to its fullest and enjoy every blessing God affords me to engage.

I AM EMBRACING NEW RELATIONSHIPS THAT CHALLENGE ME TO BE BETTER THAN I AM TODAY.

RELATIONSHIPS (BENEFICIAL)

Who are you?

It's a thin line between success and failure. I understand that one of the determining factors in this boils down to who I allow into my life. I thought I knew what was best for me, but my way keeps leaving me in situations that hinder my progress. So I am now leaving it up to God to send the people that I need in my life. I will know this time for sure because I won't make a decision without thinking it through. My future is important to me, so the people that I embrace have no choice but to align with my Purpose and Destiny.

My Prayer

Father, I thank you for Your wisdom that consistently allows me to know who's in my life and for what reason. I thank You that you have already ordained those persons who have been assigned to my purpose and my destiny. I thank You that I will mistake a beneficial relationship for an intruder because of past experiences. I choose to allow you to lead, guide, and order my steps in the direction that You already have planned for me. In Jesus Name, Amen.

My Declaration

I declare that I am connected to World Changers. I declare that the people that I will embrace in this next season will be instrumental in getting me to my next place of Success. I declare that I shall not lose time and waste valuable energy on any person who does not align with my purpose. I declare that I am alert concerning every conversation and word spoken into my life. I declare that I will not miss my moment!

THE TRUTH

It is a true statement that nothing in life comes free. Because of this truth, I have learned to always stay alert especially when it comes to my dreams. There is always a secret agent awaiting to detour me away from achieving my goal. I understand that anything that has success written on it automatically becomes a target for attacks. Success will never be accomplished with adversity. I have an enemy. My Destiny has an enemy. My Purpose has an enemy. I have notice at times I have been the enemy. But I now set my mind to the highest form of alertness so that I may clearly see what's ahead of me.

I HAVE AN ENEMY THAT LIES IN WAIT TO STEAL MY SUCCESS.

THE ENEMY OF SUCCESS

My Enemy Won't Win!

I appreciate every person who has spoken positive declarations over my life and future. But I also have the understanding to know that something's will not be conquered without a fight. I also understand that my fight is not against a human body form. I have made up my mind that I want my success so bad that I'm willing to risk it all. I will fight to the end because I know a champion lives on the inside of me, and I refuse to quit when I am this close to the finish line! I see my enemy for who and what it is and I've set my heart to WIN.

My Prayer

Father, thank you for giving me the Power of Discernment. I thank you for aligning my will with your will. I thank you that I will not be defeated because you are standing with me as well as fighting for me. I thank you God for strength to stand in the times of adversities and challenges. I thank you that my VICTORY IS SURE! I am grateful for the opportunity to stand and represent you in a dark world. Thank you for always being my Protector and Shield. I thank you that you know what's best for me and my enemies don't stand a chance against you! In Jesus Name, Amen.

My Declaration

I declare that I am strong of a good courage. I declare that I am alert to all distractions. I declare that I will not become comfortable upon arriving to this blessed place. I declare that I shall stay prayerful and watchful for anything that may come to hinder, deceive, dismantle, or disrupt my journey to victory. I declare that I am a winner. I declare that as of this moment no attack shall overtake me because I fight with faith and wisdom. I declare that my success is secured.

THE TRUTH

I have finally gotten to the place where I am able to focus all of my energy on the assignment. Many things are coming at me right now to cloud my judgment and shake my faith. Fear is the opposite of Faith. There was a time in my life where I cared about everything people said about me, but since that time I've matured! I understand that I will not be able to change the perception of everyone I come into contact with, but I can make sure the impression I leave is a positive one. I know I will continue to run into things on this journey that I have no control over but I do have control over how I respond. I am approaching every situation with an optimistic view. I am making a promise to myself that I will let nothing distract me or steal my focus. When it seems as if it's about to become overwhelming, I will just do what I do best.... Soar Above My Distractions.

I DON'T BOW TO THE STORM

– I SOAR ABOVE THE STORM.

SOARING ABOVE DISTRACTIONS

No, Not This Time

I keep saying to myself, I've fought this battle so many times and lost, but this time I've learned my lesson. I have learned the only way to beat distractions is not to respond to them. When I respond to the distraction, I give it power to become bigger. The distraction is after me, I'm not after it. I am an eagle and eagles don't give in to the storm, they simply rise above it. I am not going to waste another day worrying about what type of affect a trial or circumstance will have on me. If a storm wants to find me it will have to soar to where I am, and even if it reaches me it only forces me to soar higher. My distractions are simple placement reminders. They remind me that I'm soaring lower than where I was originally designed.

My Prayer

Father, I thank you for allowing me to see peace in the midst of any storm that may encounter. I know that you are the Anchor of my soul, therefore I don't have to fear. I thank you that you are teaching me patience and humility through my storm. I thank you that when it seems like the storm and distractions are going to get the best of me, you then become the wind beneath my wings. I soar above my distractions because you are the strength I need to do so. In Jesus Name, Amen.

My Declaration

I declare that my focus is secure. I declare that I am not bowing to my circumstances. I declare that I am gaining momentum as I go through my daily life to live my nest life now. I declare that my mindset is being upgraded. I declare that I am able to soar above any challenge that comes my way. I declare that I see myself a victor and not a victim. I declare that I shall not be defeated, detoured, or delayed because of distractions. I declare that my distractions are not my reality but they serve as an indication that I am on the right track.

THE TRUTH

If I were to be honest with myself, I haven't always been this excited about my dreams. I have been in a state of mind so contrary to success that if someone didn't come along and speak a word of life to me I would have given up a long time ago. So, not that I'm in a very vital point in my life, what's wrong with doing for someone what someone did for me. I am not egotistical, bias, or arrogant. I am going to use what little knowledge I have acquired to help someone else. I'm not the only one with a dream, and just like I needed encouragement so does someone else. I have learned many lessons on this journey and if God put me here to be a light in a dark world, it needs to start one person at a time.

I AM GIVING TO OTHERS WHAT OTHERS GAVE TO ME!

ENCOURAGE SOMEONE

It's Really Not About Me Anymore

It is impossible to accomplish any major task alone. I am not a one-man army. I have to take the time to show people how important encouragement really is. Yes, I am able to encourage myself but it feels good to hear it from someone else. So if I feel that way, how does the person feel that maybe waiting for a word of encouragement from me. I was placed on earth to be a help to my brothers and sisters of all nationalities. This journey is so much bigger than me. I want to be to others what others have been to me. I was placed here to be a light, a source of hope, and display of God in the earth. So I will never become too busy to stop and tell someone *"You can make it."* I am encouraged today because someone lifted my spirits by their words, so I will do the same.

My Prayer

Father, it is my prayer that you help me to know when someone is down and needs a lift in their spirits. I've been there before and I know how it feels. So I thank you for allowing me to cross paths with people who need to experience and be reminded of your unfailing love for them. I Thank you for making my life an example of love and teaching me how to see people the way you do. God, continue to make me a better encourager. In Jesus Name, Amen.

My Declaration

I declare that every life I come in contact with is changed for the better. I declare that I will not became so busy to where I miss an opportunity to help my fellow brother or sister. I declare that my words are life. I declare that I will speak only those things that uplift the heart, bring clarity to the weary and peace to the troubled soul. I declare that I am an Encourager. I declare that I will display and walk in the love of God throughout the earth.

THE TRUTH

Well go figure, when I get one thing taken care of all of a sudden I get questions about how did I get here? Well I don't know! I'm still trying to figure it out myself. Don't get me wrong, I'm really excited but to know that God treats me with unexpected favors is not something I can explain. I've been trying to figure this out for a while now. I don't control how He operates but I do know that what He does is beyond words.

So, I can't tell you how He does it, or why He does things that makes people wonder about me, but I will say that I'm enjoying every bit of it. Why am I going to apologize for what's taken place...I really don't know how to? I just know that whatever is going on right now, I don't ever want it to stop! There are certainly benefits to being connected with royalty. Things the normal person has to work for just drops in my lap...so how do I respond? I don't! There is nothing I can do about it.

THERE ARE BENEFITS THAT COME WITH BEING CONNECTED TO ROYALTY.

FAVOR HAS NEVER BEEN FAIR

How Am I Suppose To Explain This?

Who Are you? What Do You Do? Where Did You Come From? You name it I've been asked. I'm like I should be asking you the same thing. I am wondering why they are so intrigued by me and they don't know I'm more so intrigued by them. They are thinking I'm something big and I'm like what do you see and then it hit me- **THEY SEE THE FAVOR!** The Favor that gives you things you definitely didn't work for. So when they ask those questions of suspense and curiosity, I just tell them, I'm one of His favorites. I don't have any type of special wand or magical tricks to perform, all I have is Him. And from the looks of it, He's all I will ever need. His Favor is Priceless.

My Prayer

Father, I just want to take this moment to thank you for you favor. It has literally made my life the talk of the world! I knew you had something up your sleeves when you chose me, but never in a million years did I think I would be in this place. I would be crazy to say I did this on my own, and actually saying it's just a blessing is an understatement. you have literally outdone yourself and for that I appreciate you. Don't let me take this moment of favor lightly. It's because of you I am what I am. Thank you for keeping your word. In Jesus, Amen.

My Declaration

I declare that I walk in Supernatural and Unexplainable Favor. I declare that this Favor is opening doors for me no man can shut. I declare that the favor on my life becomes contagious to all that support and believe in me. I declare that this Favor shall bring overwhelming wealth and riches so that we can further help mankind. I declare that every person I come in contact with will encourage others as we walk out on purpose on earth. I declare Favor is my daily portion.

NOTES TO SELF

A Personal Note From Andy

In the day we are living in, everyone wants to be connected. Once upon a time, I was a person who carried that same ambition. I begin finding myself time and time again being put in places where I wasn't wanted or needed. It is so easy these days to get involved and tangled in relationships that have no investment in our purpose. When you get to the point where you are known for being a spotlight driven person, it has gone too far. Non-beneficial relationships have you constantly giving and never being a recipient.

I had to learn the hard way that when you collide with God-ordained relationships they just click. As they begin to grow and develop, you begin to notice a difference in the investments. Beneficial relationships give as much to you as you give to them. When you meet people who are willing to sacrifice their time and efforts to pour knowledge and wisdom into you dream or idea, it is very important that you protect the relationship. There is always an enemy of success seeking to destroy anything that has your best interest at heart. Always remain alert to who you allow in your circle.

When you begin discovering who you were created to be, beware of the people who pop up just to give you reasons why your idea is not a good one. I am not talking about those who bring a balancing perspective, I mean those who basically have nothing positive to say. I had to learn to square my shoulders and stand on faith. I never gave a person the pleasure of knowing that they were successful in filling my heart and spirit with fear. It simply taught me the lesson to be careful who I share my dreams with. Everybody doesn't want to see you succeed.

Distractions come in many ways. Discernment is key. I would find myself so distracted at times to where I literally forgot what I was working on. I am a Social Media Guru, but it has also served as a distraction. I would wake up in the morning and surf, all through the day and late at night, and before I knew it I had accomplished absolutely nothing. An important detail in self-discovery is knowing your strengths and weaknesses. If you're not careful you will begin to major in minor and minor in the major. Distractions only come to detour and delay you. But like me, I was able to be honest with myself and fix the problem.

Self-Discovery carries its benefits and burdens. One of the benefits is called Favor! Favor allows you access to things everybody else cannot encounter. It may even sometime seem unfair the way God allows you to excel in your dream, but it does feel good. Favor will have you thinking that you're God's favorite person in the whole wide world, and in a sense you are! You will find Favor in God-ordained connections. It doesn't matter how many people tell you no, there will always be that one person who says yes! That's the important of being connected to the right people.

CHAPTER FIVE
THE UNSTOPPABLE VISION
The Power Of Faith In Action

THE TRUTH

I just realized that this process is only what I make it. It would be easy for me to approach my new season with an old mindset because it's what I'm used to. But I am choosing to look at things in a new way. It's not hard for me to find a reason to stop and quit right now, but like the old saying says..." Winners Never Quit...and...Quitters Never Win." So if I am going to win in this new season of my life, the way I see myself matters. I am making the choice to see the glass half full rather than half empty. My way of thinking is changing starting today. I am convinced even more now that I was created to succeed! So I will let nothing shake my faith in who I was created to be. I am approaching all assignments with a positive and optimistic perspective.

I SEE THE GLASS HALF FULL RATHER THAN HALF EMPTY!

A FRESH PERSPECTIVE

Take Another Look

I am becoming more and more excited about the fact that God's going to use me to change someone's life. (Jeremiah 29:11) I was thinking about all of the mistakes I've made in my past and I started to feel like this shift was impossible. I even started to replay some of the things that were spoken of over me, and then I remembered that no one has the power to change the way I see me if I don't allow them to. So I decided to remind myself of the reason why I was born. I was born to be a testimony of Grace and Redemption. So when I feel myself getting discouraged, I just take another look at my future and all doubts begin to fly out the window.

My Prayer

Father, I thank you for giving me a second wind and fresh vision. Thank you that discouragement did not set in and begin to ruin your desires for my life. I ask that you always keep reminded that my life is not my own. I want to fulfill every assignment that you've placed in my heart. I want to die empty. So thank you for never allowing me to settle in what I think is a situation of doom. I see greater for my life. In Jesus Name, Amen.

My Declaration

I declare that my vision is clear. I declare my perceptions and perspectives are precise and full of faith and excitement. I will not allow fear to enter my mind and force out my ability to believe for what some call the impossible. I am seeing my future more clearly than I've seen before in my life. My vision has RESET.

THE TRUTH

I often wonder what keeps my head on straight when everything around me seems unstable? I don't know what tomorrow holds and at this point it's not even important. I am focused on my today and more so than ever I have a passion for what I do and who I am. My passion for success has become a force to be reckoned with! I won't ever conquer my assignment with a mindset of failure and mediocrity. I am passionate about fulfilling my purpose so therefore I will allow nothing to stop me from pushing past the hard knocks of life. I am standing strong in faith knowing that I am focused, fervent, and faithful to my dreams. I have a passion that will not under any circumstances die out!

MY PASSION FOR MY DREAM HAS BECOME MY SECRET WEAPON.

THE AWAKENING OF MY PASSION

My Passion has come Alive!

Something is taken place on the inside of me that I've never felt before. It feels like a baby is leaping and I have an indescribable fire burning in me that's thrusting me into another dimension. I can't really put it into words but I do know my dream has come alive and I am ready to experience this new place. I am overwhelmingly excited to know that what I only once dreamed about as an impossible thing is now becoming a present reality.

My Prayer

Father, it is with a sincere heart I say to you that your love for me blows my mind. There have been times when I never would have saw myself in this place. you have been more than faithful to me and I am so grateful. Thank you God for never giving up on me. I thank you for seeing in me what I could not see in myself. God, thank you for this new found fire that only you could ignite in me. you are like none other, and you keep proving yourself every day. Thank you for loving me despite of myself. In Jesus Name, Amen.

My Declaration

I declare that I will never allow my passion for my dreams to die. I declare that I am about to experience the reason why I was born. I declare that success is my portion and I shall see the fruits of my labor in this season of my life. I declare that I am the blessed of God and everything I touch is sealed with Prosperity and Favor. I declare that my passion has been ignited and will never be quenched.

THE TRUTH

I have learned throughout this journey that success is common to those associate with successful people. But I also understand that there is more to it than association. I am teaching myself how to put something in the ground. How can I expect a return on an investment without an initial investment? I can't expect something from nothing. If I want to see something I've never seen, I must do something that I've never done. What good is faith without work? What good is a dream without reality? What good is it to expect a harvest without a seed? I am telling myself every day that I will reap what I sow, so I am making it my business only to plant in this life what I want to come up. The seeds I plant I will see again so I will plant seeds of encouragement and support as much as possible, because I will need the harvest to reflect what I've sown.

WHAT GOOD IS IT TO EXPECT A HARVEST WHEN THERE HAS BEEN NO SEED?

THE GROUND MATTERS

What Goes Down Will Come Up

Who understands more about putting into your dream than me? I've seen myself in some amazing places and traveling the world. I've also seen myself doing something's that made absolutely no sense whatsoever when it comes to investing in future. I knew that it would take stepping on in a way that no one would understand. So what did I do, I started putting things I would need in the ground. I started giving to people what I would need on my journey. There is no way I could have started this journey towards success and not put seeds in the ground along the way. I understand now what I plant will come up again. So I plant positive and life-changing seeds of hope and inspiration to all that I may encounter.

My Prayer

Father, I thank you for teaching me the importance of sowing good seeds. I ask you to make me aware of the people that need the seeds so that no seeds can be wasted. I thank you for allowing me to see the harvest of some of the seeds that have been planted. I know that a bigger harvest is on the way. I thank you for allowing be to be a blessing and encouragement in the lives of so many people. I thank you that every seed that I sow I will seed again. In Jesus, Amen.

My Declaration

I declare that I am blessed to be a blessing. I declare that I will never pass up an opportunity to sow a seed in someone else's life. I declare that I shall experience my harvest in this season of my life. I declare that my life is a testimony of positive seeds. I declare that I will teach others the importance of putting something in the ground as others have taken the time to teach me. I declare that all of the seeds plant in the lives of other shall be paid forward for generations to come. I declare that every person that sows into my life shall be blessed beyond measures. I declare that my seeds are eternal blessings.

THE TRUTH

I am enjoying this journey, but why must I encounter people who are sent to just frustrate me? I know they don't understand what I've been called to do, but just because they don't understand it doesn't mean I want to hear their opinion about it. I am in full bulldozer mode when it comes to people dropping off their negativity in my life. I don't want to hear about any problems unless they have a solution. I have enough problems of my own. I have to be sure not to let my guards down and get comfortable around people, because I don't want my kindness to be mistaken for weakness. I love to laugh but I am serious about my success and if you get in my way I will run you over. My fight is different; I've had to pay a dear price to get it so don't waste my time with games.

I'VE PAID A DEAR PRICE TO GET HERE!

YOU'VE BEEN WARNED

Don't Get In My Way

Do I give off the aroma that I encourage negativity? Of course not! I am determined to see my dream become a reality and I will not allow anyone to stop it. I know I may have to suck up a few denials before it's over but I will not bow to rejection. I have the faith that I can speak to any mountain whether it be a situation or a person and cause it to become non-existent. I have a boldness that stands up it me that some may mistake for arrogance, but that's not it. I am bold and confidence because I know who I am and what I've been called to accomplish. If I feel that there is a potential threat to my future I, then transform into a madman. I don't want to offend anyone. I want to remain humble. I refuse to submit to an unhealthy environment so if they are not serious about success they need to simple GET OUT OF MY WAY.

My Prayer

Father, I thank you for placing on the inside of me a boldness that stands second to none. I thank you that I am confident in what you have placed in my heart for this generation of people. I thank you that you will not allow me to associate, connect, or lock arms with any person who has secret intentions to hinder my Destiny. I thank you that I am more focused than I've ever been. I thank you that you have given me power to press through any situation set up against me. I boast in you, because the fire of success I carry is fueled by you. Thank you for giving me boldness! In Jesus, Amen.

My Declaration

I declare that I carry the boldness of A Lion. I declare that my strength can never be weaken by mediocrity. I declare that I have the boldness to set straight any naysayer if I have to without offense and fear. I declare that I am serious about my assignment and only associate with those who are serious about theirs. I declare that boldness is my secret weapon.

THE TRUTH

I am really excited for some reason but also super nervous. I didn't know how

I would feel once I got here, but now that I'm here, I have mixed emotions. As I look back on this process of effectively evaluating my life, tough becomes an understatement. Today I take a detailed look into how far I've come, the lessons I've learned, as well as what's I've accomplished on the way here. I am grateful for everything I have been through and everything I didn't have to go through. I have learned something's about myself that I know. I have survived some storms I didn't know I had the strength to endure. So what do I do now, I stop. I don't stop because I have arrived, not I still have a long way to go, but I'm stopping so I can celebrate what has taken place knowing that the best is yet to come. So I stop now to just breathe and back to work I go.

I AM STOPPING NOT BECAUSE I HAVE ARRIVED – ONLY TO CELEBRATE THIS MOMENT

TAKE A MOMENT TO BREATHE

The Time Has Finally Come

Where Am I? Am I There Yet? It would be nice to tell myself that, but sorry that's not the case. I know that the journey has been long for me but I still haven't seen all of the things that I want to see manifest in my life. I am excited about the progress I've made, but the journey is far from over. So I'm going to use a little wisdom here and just pause for a moment and BREATHE. It's okay for me to work hard and be aggressive, but I also need to know when to rest. If I rest, it doesn't mean that I'm quitting or losing momentum, it simply means that I'm bracing myself for the next phase of this journey.

My Prayer

Father, I thank you for how far I've come, and where you are taking me. I thank you for giving me such a powerful push in my spirit to go after my dreams. I thank you that you are helping me use wisdom in when it's time to take a break and regroup. This journey can become overwhelming at times but you have already figured that into the road towards success. So I take a moment and I rest in you knowing you're going to give me my next step and where to go from here. I thank you for giving me a new burst of energy not only in my physical body but also in my mind, heart, and spirit. In Jesus, Amen.

My Declaration

I declare that I am using wisdom when it comes to my dream. I declare that I shall not burn out on the way to my destined place. I declare that I will take advantage of the important things such as rest and relaxation. I declare that I am simply regaining strength for the next assignment on this journey. I declare that I am renewed in my mind, heart, and spirit. I declare that I shall stand firm in this assignment knowing I have taken the necessary steps to remain in the race.

THE TRUTH

Okay that was a run for the history books, but the only problem is there is so much more on the inside of me. I thought I was going to get here and chill and take it easy, no are you crazy? What was I thinking? I have another assignment brewing, and I know this journey will never end until the day I stop breathing. I can't stop here! I won't stop here! I fought long and hard to see this vision to come to reality, and now here comes another one. Wow! I guess I know what it means now to embrace the next level. I thought I did well, but something keeps pushing me to climb higher. I was telling myself "the sky is the limit" and now I see when it comes to being successful there is no sky! So, I guess I'll square my shoulders once again, get in the race, and do it all over again.

WHEN IT COMES TO BEING SUCCESSFUL THERE IS NO SKY!

LET'S START OVER

Embracing The Next Level

After many nights of sleepless nights, uncontrollable tears and frustration, I finally get to the place where I can see the fruits of my labor. Many have told me okay, you did well that's enough, but I beg to differ. I have so many dreams on the inside that I want to see become a reality, so stopping here at this point doesn't make sense. I am ready to see even more greater things take place in my life and the lives of those connected to me. So, after seeing one vision come to reality, it's is time to do it all over again. I have my Faith, my confidence, my drive, and my God. I am ready to climb higher than I've ever gone before. I am ready to embrace my next level. I am excited cause I get to do it all over again!

My Prayer

Father, I thank you for this journey. I thank you for what I have encountered along the way. you have allowed me to meet so many amazing people, and to learn so many amazing things. I often wonder where would my life be if I hadn't jumped? It hasn't been the easiest road, but it has definitely been worth it. I am watching my life unfold and watching things you've promised to me come to reality. I am so grateful that you love me enough to bless my life. I thank you that even more because you are about to give me the wisdom and strength to do it again. I want to die empty. I plan to fulfill my purpose to its maximum potential and accomplished everything you've created me to do. Okay, I'm ready...Let's Do It Again! In Jesus, Amen.

My Declaration

I declare that I shall embrace the next season of my life with joy! I declare that I have a new passion for this next season and a new excitement. I declare that I shall use everything I've learned on this journey and apply it to my new assignment. I declare that I have yet to see my greatest days. I declare that this fresh start shall lead me to even greater avenues of success. I declare that my best days are ahead of me and I am just getting started.

NOTES TO SELF

_____

_____

_____

_____

_____

_____

_____

_____

_____

_____

_____

_____

_____

_____

A Personal Note From Andy

Have you ever felt like you were on the brink of something big? I've noticed that something's are more difficult to explain than others. I find it hard to explain the excitement that I sense not only for me but you as well! After finally going through the process of changing this and re-evaluating that, it's safe to say that you now have a new perspective on your future. I can truly say I don't see myself the same anymore. I have finally discovered the real me! It may have taken some time, but I am now on the right track, and ready to see what life has in store for me.

When I finally discovered who I really was, it was like something awakened in me! It was like a force that I have never seen or felt before. I begin to write it down the best way I could what I was feeling, the words were few. But after careful research, I was able to successfully pinpoint what took place, my passion was revived! It was like I was a new person, and I felt like I could leap over buildings. I finally discovered who I was always meant to be. I followed the instructions given to me and I came out a winner.

What we must realize is once we put the seed in the ground, we must water it with discipline, prayer, and a strong work ethic. You cannot expect to get a harvest from a seed without work. God will take care of the harvest, if you would just keep planting. I start telling myself that all my hard work would pay off. I am now in position for the blessing.

It's to stop and breathe, but never stop striving to get to your destiny. The road to Success is very crowded, but the journey of Self-Discovery is an audience of one. The way you see yourself will determine the way others see you. If you walk around with low self-esteem nobody will take you seriously. But, I encourage you to approach every new day as the day that your dream just may become a reality. There is no set date on when you'll reach your destiny, but when you do, you will know it and most of all so will those watching you.

Just in case you haven't realized it yet, the journey to discovery who you were created to be has already begun. I am proud of myself for taking the first step to understanding my role in the earth, and you should be too! Now, it's time to get up and make a difference. You have been endowed with endless possibilities to leave your mark here on earth. So what are you waiting on? You're the coach, the player, and the cheerleader - now get up and score. The world is waiting for you. Because you have taken the time to look deep within yourself to locate your creative being, there is nothing else stopping you. You have now been discovered.

AUTHOR BIOGRAPHY

But now bring me a minstrel. And it came to pass, when the minstrel played, that the hand of the LORD came upon him." 2 Kings 3:15

From the foundations of the world it was predestined that Andy Smith be called into the Kingdom and World for such a time as this. It was always spoken that he would impact the world because of His love for God and God's people. God has taken a young, ordinary man and entrusted in him an extraordinary anointing through the ministry of Worship which is literally tearing down barriers and destroying the yokes of bondage across the United States.

Andy Smith is fulfilling his purpose

and passion in the Kingdom as one of God's end-time prophetic voices. As he travels from ministry to ministry releasing the power of God by way of workshops, conferences and seminars, lives are changed, bodies healed, souls saved and purposes are revealed as God Encounters are invoked all over the land.

Andy Smith is a Chief Minstrel and faithful member of the Walk In The Word Church in Monroe, LA where the Honorable Bishop Danny C. and Dr. Carolyn Hunt serve as Senior Pastors. He thanks God for his accomplishments, trials, successes, and failures. He accredits most of his attributed learning to the years of service given in his community.

Smith has been graced to host and Annual Praise & Worship Conference in

Northeast LA which ministers to needs of the local church strengthening their musicians and worship leaders by informative information and Prophetic Impartation. Smith is the author of the new Book Release "The Lost Worshipper" The Passions, Pressures, & Powers Of A Worship Leader. Smith is also the Director of The I-Worship Network, a full-service Branding & Marketing Network, which consist of a Master-Class and National Magazine.

Smith has ministry at heart and he carries an undeniable grace that consistently allows him to tap the vein of God through worship and proclaim the acceptable year of the Lord.

CONTACT INFORMATION

Andy Smith Monroe
Mailing Address: P.O. BOX 4623
MONROE, LA 71211

Phone: 800.311.4045
Email: asmithmonroe@gmail.com
Website: www.andysmithmonroe.com

Facebook
Twitter
Instagram
Periscope
@AndySmithMonroe

63590806R00091

Made in the USA
Charleston, SC
05 November 2016